To the kids in my family—and all those in yours:
hoping they enjoy these poems by William Blake.
—J.M.
A mio padre.
—A.C.

Library of Congress Cataloging-in-Publication Data

Blake, William, 1757-1827.
[Poems. Selections]
William Blake / edited by John Maynard ; illustrated by Alessandra Cimatoribus.
p. cm. — (Poetry for young people)
Includes index.
ISBN-13: 978-0-8069-3647-5
ISBN-10: 0-8069-3647-9
1. Children's poetry, English. I. Maynard, John, 1941- II. Cimatoribus, Alessandra, ill. III.
Title. IV. Series.
PR4142.M39 2006
821'.7—dc22   2006013858

The drawing of William Blake (ca, 1825) by John Linnell on page 4 is used with the kind permission of the Fitzwilliam
Museum, Cambridge, England. The illustrations from Songs of Innocence and Experience and The Song of Los on
pages 6, 7, and 8 are courtesy of The Rosenwald Collection, The Library of Congress.

2 4 6 8 10 9 7 5 3 1

Published by Sterling Publishing Co., Inc.
387 Park Avenue South, New York, NY 10016
Editorial text © 2006 by John Maynard
Illustrations © 2006 by Alessandra Cimatoribus
Distributed in Canada by Sterling Publishing
^c/o Canadian Manda Group, 165 Dufferin Street
Toronto, Ontario, Canada M6K 3H6
Distributed in the United Kingdom by GMC Distribution Services
Castle Place, 166 High Street, Lewes, East Sussex, England BN7 1XU
Distributed in Australia by Capricorn Link (Australia) Pty. Ltd.
P.O. Box 704, Windsor, NSW 2756, Australia

Printed in China
All rights reserved

Sterling ISBN-13: 978-0-8069-3647-5
ISBN-10: 0-8069-3647-9

For information about custom editions, special sales, premium and
corporate purchases, please contact Sterling Special Sales
Department at 800-805-5489 or specialsales@sterlingpub.com.

Contents

Introduction 4

from *Songs of Innocence*

The Shepherd 10
The Ecchoing Green 11
The Lamb 12
The Chimney Sweeper 14
The Little Boy Lost 15
The Little Boy Found 16
The Divine Image 17
Night 18
Nurse's Song 20
A Dream 21
On Another's Sorrow 22

from *Songs of Experience*

The Clod & the Pebble 24
Holy Thursday 25
from The Little Girl Lost 26
The Little Girl Found 28
The Chimney Sweeper 30
Nurse's Song 31

The Sick Rose 32
The Angel 33
The Tyger 34
Ah! Sun-Flower 35
The Garden of Love 36
Infant Sorrow 37
A Poison Tree 38
A Little Boy Lost 39
The School Boy 40

from *The Marriage of Heaven and Hell* 42

from *Jerusalem: The Emanation of the Giant Albion* 44

from Auguries of Innocence 45

from *Milton* 46

from To Thomas Butts, October 2, 1800 47

Index 48

INTRODUCTION

The report we hear from everyone who knew William Blake or has known his works is that he was truly remarkable, an exceptional person. And that is true even among poets and artists, who are so often considered to be very special people. For one thing Blake seems to have been a genius first, a poet and an artist second. He certainly was in fact both poet and artist, one of England's really great poets—England produced many fine poets—and also one of her greatest artists, a major figure among not too many. He was a very fine craftsman who thought of his poetry and art work as going together into beautiful creations. In rare book libraries you can still see the precious decorated pages of printing in which he presented his poetry and art all together. He was a hard-working man who did his own production, a maker of fine printed works.

He was also a thinker, someone who insisted on going his own way in his approach to the world. He is famous for saying that he had to create his own world of thought himself and not take anything handed down from other thinkers. He figured it out this way: "I must Create a System, or be enslav'd by another Man's." (Writers in his time often capitalized words they considered important.) That sounds easy enough, but it is an almost incredibly difficult task. We all take our view of the world from those around us, and Blake of course began by doing so too. But he struggled all his life to examine all that he heard and read and to develop his own strong view of things. It wasn't enough just to have his own ideas and thoughts about everything. He wanted more. He wanted to develop his own mythology, his own way of thinking and feeling about the entire universe and man's place in it. Above all, he wanted to portray man at his best as the center of the universe, a four-fold combination of wisdom, love, imagination, and strength. Blake was a mythmaker; in both his poetry and his art he created a whole set of figures with brave new names to give body to his thinking.

In developing his myths Blake had help that was truly exceptional. All his life he believed he could make direct contact with creatures of another world. This was not science fiction but his special experience of religion. When he was four, he had a vision of God, and later he saw a tree full of angels in a field near London. When his brother, whom he loved, died of illness when Blake was thirty, he saw the spirit of his brother ascending to heaven through the ceiling and clapping its hands for joy. He said he was the companion of angels and sometimes spoke of himself as a writer who merely served as secretary for them, writing down what they dictated. When he himself came to die at age sixty-nine, he happily sang songs about what he saw in heaven. While some people called him the mad Blake, most who knew him found him always sincere and clear, merely that he had visions constantly of what others could not see. He spoke of them in a very matter-of-fact way without any wildness or even wish to persuade others of what he saw. He imagined someone asking him about his different vision: "'What,' it will be Questiond, 'When the sun rises, do you not see a round disk of fire somewhat like a Guinea?' O no, no, I see an Innumerable company of the Heavenly host crying 'Holy, Holy, Holy is the Lord God Almighty.' I question not my Corporeal . . . Eye any more than I would Question a Window concerning a Sight: I look thro it & not with it." He asserted that he had visions of eternity. He was a Christian—but after his own fashion—and mixed ideas of Christ as the central man on whom everyone depended with his own set of mythological persons representing different human qualities. So his myth-making was in the end a form of his own religion. He insisted that there was much more in the world of man than what ordinary people can see and he wanted to open up that world to others by his work. Not much respected on earth, he claimed he was in heaven a "Prince among Princes."

As a man, Blake was also remarkable. He worked at his art with great effort all his life. He didn't care about making money and never thought much about selling his work for great prices; nor did he have much regard for luxury of any sort. He lived like a simple workman, usually in a basic room or, once when he spent a time in the country, in a very plain cottage. An acquaintance said he was "a man without a mask; his aim single, his path straight-forwards, and his wants few; so he was free, noble, and happy." He was not a tall man, but he was very powerful. Once a soldier who had been drinking too much gave him difficulty, and he virtually carried the man away from his house without allowing any kind of fighting. The soldier tried to pretend that Blake was committing treason against the state, but no one would believe him against the good word of this hard-working craftsman, and the court set him free. He was said to be patient as a lamb, able to roar like a lion, but with none of the serpent's sneakiness. He loved and protected children. He made friends and kept his friends. There were a few people who loved his work and were there to help him out if he ran into difficulties. To them he wrote warm and very interesting letters about his life and his plans for his work. And there was his wife. In his youth, he had been in love with a woman who would take no interest in him. He told someone else about this, and she felt so bad for him that she told him so. In turn, he was so happy that she cared about his pain that he decided she was a better person to love. They were married and were an unusually happy couple who were constantly together until the day he died. His wife, whose name was Catherine, worked beside him in his art and shared his private dreams and visions.

Blake was highly respected by the few people who knew him well. Everyone who did was struck by his remarkable single-mindedness and devotion to his work. He was never in any way famous, and he was not much known by the next generation of poets, artists, and readers. Although he was similar to some of the other Romantic poets of his time (about 1800–1825) in his interest in myth and his concern that poetry should express a personal vision, he was also very much ahead of them. He scorned most of the thinkers who were then highly respected. He did not care to look at the world as a machine, and he thought language was not given to people to do business, but to get in touch with their inner selves. His art was not careful and perfected, but vibrant and fantastic, visionary art. Eventually newer generations began to discover the special power of this man's work. Instead of being a curiosity known to only a few people, he came to be the favorite poet or artist, or both, for young creative people. His shorter poems have become favorites for readers everywhere and his longer poems a special study of people looking for a new kind of thinker who could imagine a new kind of society and human nature. He became a kind of prophet, someone who would renew people's understanding of important values in life. So two hundred years and more after his birth, Blake has come into his full fame. What seemed so remarkable, but also strange to his time, has been recognized as still remarkable but very much for our time.

Blake was born in London in 1757 to a shopkeeper family. His father was a hosier, which means someone who sells stockings and underwear. Blake had obvious ability as an artist

Blake's frontispiece to Songs of Innocence, *1794*

Blake's frontispiece to Songs of Experience, *1794*

even as a boy, and he was given a chance to go to drawing school. As an apprentice to a practicing one, he learned to be an engraver, someone who cut or etched artwork into solid stone or metal or wood so that the work could be printed over and over again. Blake worked very hard at his engravings, both for his own work and for other books and subjects. This was a regular craft, but it was also a fine art, and Blake took a great interest in the great artists of the past, especially Michelangelo, Leonardo, and Raphael. They made the human form the center of their work, and he determined to do the same. The strong figures of men and women are remarkable in his work; he makes their inner strength and energy speak in the pictures of their bodies. And he also creates bodies that talk about the limits and pains of some people's inner lives. If you like to draw people, you can learn a great deal from Blake.

Blake had to focus on art because that was the craft he was learning in order to support himself. He didn't have regular high school or university education, but he loved to read. He got himself a major education reading on his own. He was exceptionally well read in English, and he also learned classical languages in order to read Greek, Latin, and Hebrew in the original. Later he learned French and Italian. He loved John Milton, who wrote the great English epic *Paradise Lost,* based on the first book of the Bible, and Blake loved the Bible itself. His reading and his natural independence of mind brought him to his own positions on nearly every subject. When he read a book, he often talked back to the author, agreeing or sometimes strongly disagreeing with him or her by vigorous comments in the margins. Many writers do this (not with library books!) because they think about what they read and how they feel about it—they read and they write. And indeed much of Blake's writing is a rewriting of works he had read. He even wrote an epic named after his favorite writer, Milton.

Blake's best known and best loved poems are the shorter ones he wrote for children and grownups alike. He called them *Songs of Innocence and Songs of Experience* (published together by him in 1794, though they had appeared separately earlier), and as with most of his poetry, he produced them in volumes beautifully illustrated by himself. He did the engraving on copper plates and then usually colored in the prints that he made. When you see them, you can see that his coloring is as special and striking as his figures. (You can see several here in the Introduction and others on the Web at http://www.loc.gov/rr/rarebook/rosenwald.html.) Blake's works are now extremely valuable since he only did a relatively few copies.

Blake said, "Without Contraries is no progression." What he seems to have meant is that life is filled with opposites and we learn best by accepting that as a fundamental reality. He speaks of oppositions such as love and hate, reason and energy. Life is given tension and is filled with energies when we let all the forces within us find expression. When one part becomes too powerful there is danger. Most often the danger is that there is too much control: the adult wins out over the child, the society over the individual, laws over people's wishes. In his later, prophetic work Blake will even create a bad mythic figure, Urizen (possibly your reason) to embody this repressive overcontrol, though he opposes him to the figure Orc, who embodies free energy. In the *Songs of Innocence and Experience,* Blake lets both contraries exist. There is a world of innocent joy which he connects to young people and (often also) young animals. This is innocence. Only it isn't just that these are innocent creatures but that the poet who speaks of them sees the world with the same innocence. His songs are in simple, lovely language, often the language of lullabies, or fairy tales, or happy tunes. The poet who sings the songs of experience (he is called a

from The Song of Los, *1795*

8

bard, which makes us think of old poets with great beards and a great deal to say about the complicated lives of men and nations) is only too aware that there are those who oppose such innocence. The bard is not himself against children and animals, but he knows the world has bad experiences and dangerous realities. There are lambs and there are tigers. The forms of poetry that he uses mirror those of the poetry of innocence, but they now often contain a bitter core or an ironic perception set against that of the innocent creatures. Both poets, in effect these two sides of the poet Blake, give us a full sense of what we and life are like. He knows how lovely and wonderful and loving it can be, and he knows how ugly, repressive, and hateful it can also be. And people can be both. Blake himself always believed that innocence is the fully human and that experience is a world where man falls from his best self. Many people would agree with him; many would disagree. As you read through these sections, you will find some pairs of poems, the same subject seen from the view of innocence and from that of experience.

I hope you like these famous and so well loved poems too. I have given you at the end a few selections from the much more complicated prophetic books that Blake wrote when he was older. They are hard to follow, and they use very long lines of poetry instead of the simple song forms of the *Songs*. They are filled with characters like Urizen and Los with strange names and mighty concerns, either to free or enslave themselves and other people. We can see in them Blake's preoccupation with the issues of the age of revolutions, American and French, that he lived through. People were claiming their freedom from old tyrants and aristocrats, but they and their societies were also in danger of exploding into chaos in their sudden change. Blake believed in change but located the most important change inside humans themselves. These long poems have a dreamlike quality even as they suggest great battles of giants and upheavals of the earth. They are Blake's visions, and like human feelings, they are very fluid, characters changing and melting into other states of their selves or other characters. All together, they are only parts of the total, man. Blake has been called a great poet of metamorphosis, of change in form, as people were changed into animals or bushes or rivers in Greek and Roman myths. These works are hard, but they are also works you may wish to look into more when you are older. There you can go even further to share in the rare visions of this really remarkable man and artist.

from SONGS OF INNOCENCE

Songs of Innocence offer the perspective of unworldliness, trust, and innocence, often of youth; some seem spoken by an innocent person, others by a poetic speaker who looks at innocence. In his subtitle Blake called innocence and experience two "Contrary [opposing] States of the Human Soul."

THE SHEPHERD

This poem celebrates the shepherd, who appears here as a protector of innocence. Shepherds were often the subjects or the speakers of poetry called "pastoral" because it related to pasturing animals.

How sweet is the Shepherd's sweet lot,
From the morn to the evening he strays:
He shall follow his sheep all the day
And his tongue shall be filled with praise.

For he hears the lambs' innocent call,
And he hears the ewes' tender reply,
He is watchful while they are in peace,
For they know when their Shepherd is nigh.

THE ECCHOING GREEN

The young, innocent speaker celebrates spring play on the public green. The setting, as in many of these poems, is a village world that suggests an ideal of harmony among young, old, and nature.

The Sun does arise,
And make happy the skies.
The merry bells ring
To welcome the Spring.
The sky-lark and thrush,
The birds of the bush,
Sing louder around,
To the bells' chearful sound.
While our sports shall be seen
On the Ecchoing Green.

Old John with white hair
Does laugh away care,
Sitting under the oak,
Among the old folk.
They laugh at our play,
And soon they all say,
"Such, such were the joys,
When we all girls & boys,
In our youth-time were seen,
On the Ecchoing Green."

Till the little ones weary
No more can be merry.
The sun does descend,
And our sports have an end:
Round the laps of their mothers,
Many sisters and brothers,
Like birds in their nest,
Are ready for rest:
And sport no more seen,
On the darkening Green.

Ecchoing—*Echoing*
Green—*public playfield*
Sun—*Blake follows eighteenth-century practice in
    using frequent initial capitals*
chearful—*cheerful; we preserve the spelling Blake used*

THE LAMB

A child speaker talks to a lamb and tells him of God / Jesus, who is often called the Lamb.

Little Lamb who made thee?
Dost thou know who made thee?
Gave thee life & bid thee feed
By the stream & o'er the mead;
Gave thee clothing of delight,
Softest clothing wooly bright;
Gave thee such a tender voice,
Making all the vales rejoice:
Little Lamb who made thee?
Dost thou know who made thee?

Little Lamb I'll tell thee,
Little Lamb I'll tell thee:
He is called by thy name,
For he calls himself a Lamb:
He is meek & he is mild,
He became a little child:
I a child & thou a lamb,
We are called by his name.
Little Lamb God bless thee.
Little Lamb God bless thee.

Mead—*meadow*
vales—*valleys*
name—*lamb (of God, Jesus)*

THE CHIMNEY SWEEPER

The innocent speaker here, one of the little boys used mercilessly by sweepers to clear chimneys by actually going into them, has not lived a pastoral life. But he turns his harsh world into a vision of death as a release to happiness. He is then reconciled to his hard fate. Should we agree with the speaker?

When my mother died I was very young,
And my father sold me while yet my tongue
Could scarcely cry weep weep weep weep.
So your chimneys I sweep & in soot I sleep.

There's little Tom Dacre, who cried when his head
That curl'd like a lamb's back, was shav'd, so I said,
"Hush Tom never mind it, for when your head's bare,
You know that the soot cannot spoil your white hair."

And so he was quiet, & that very night,
As Tom was a sleeping he had such a sight,
That thousands of sweepers Dick, Joe, Ned & Jack
Were all of them lock'd up in coffins of black.

And by came an Angel who had a bright key,
And he open'd the coffins & set them all free.
Then down a green plain leaping laughing they run
And wash in a river and shine in the Sun.

Then naked & white, all their bags left behind,
They rise upon clouds, and sport in the wind.
And the Angel told Tom if he'd be a good boy,
He'd have God for his father & never want joy.

And so Tom awoke and we rose in the dark
And got with our bags & our brushes to work.
Tho' the morning was cold, Tom was happy & warm,
So if all do their duty, they need not fear harm.

sold—*apprenticed to a chimney sweeper*
weep—*sweep, the street cry of their
     trade, but weep fits their sad life*
wind—*wind that flows; pronounced here
     as our wind (the clock)*

THE LITTLE BOY LOST

The speaker tells us that the poor lost boy's weeping was followed by or led to the vapor flying away. Is the vapor the dew? The darkness? The clouds of life? Compare this to the next poem, "The Little Boy Found."

"Father, father, where are you going
O do not walk so fast.
Speak father, speak to your little boy
Or else I shall be lost."

The night was dark, no father was there.
The child was wet with dew.
The mire was deep, & the child did weep
And away the vapour flew.

vapour—*vapor; see the question above*

THE LITTLE BOY FOUND

God and mother rescue the lost boy.

The little boy lost in the lonely fen,
Led by the wand'ring light,
Began to cry, but God ever nigh,
Appeard like his father in white.

He kissed the child & by the hand led
And to his mother brought,
Who in sorrow pale, thro' the lonely dale
Her little boy weeping sought.

fen—*a marshy area*
wand'ring—*uncertain*
nigh—*near*
dale—*valley*

THE DIVINE IMAGE

The speaker finds the divine image, the image we have of God, is made up of the best human qualities. We should love these godly human ideals in all people who possess them.

To Mercy Pity Peace and Love,
All pray in their distress:
And to these virtues of delight
Return their thankfulness.

For Mercy Pity Peace and Love
Is God our father dear:
And Mercy Pity Peace and Love
Is Man his child and care.

For Mercy has a human heart
Pity, a human face:
And Love, the human form divine,
And Peace, the human dress.

Then every man of every clime,
That prays in his distress,
Prays to the human form divine
Love Mercy Pity Peace.

And all must love the human form,
In heathen, turk or jew.
Where Mercy, Love & Pity dwell
There God is dwelling too

NIGHT

The speaker (a shepherd?) goes home at night, but expresses trust in angels who visit sleeping creatures and, if they are killed by wild animals, usher them to the full peace of heaven.

The sun descending in the west
The evening star does shine.
The birds are silent in their nest,
And I must seek for mine.
The moon, like a flower,
In heaven's high bower,
With silent delight
Sits and smiles on the night.

Farewell green fields and happy groves,
Where flocks have took delight;
Where lambs have nibbled, silent moves
The feet of angels bright;
Unseen they pour blessing,
And joy without ceasing,
On each bud and blossom,
And each sleeping bosom.

They look in every thoughtless nest,
Where birds are covered warm;
They visit caves of every beast,
To keep them all from harm.
If they see any weeping,
That should have been sleeping,
They pour sleep on their head
And sit down by their bed.

star—*Venus*
bower—*protective enclosure*
bosom—*creature (chest taken for the whole)*

18

When wolves and tygers howl for prey
They pitying stand and weep;
Seeking to drive their thirst away,
And keep them from the sheep.
But if they rush dreadful;
The angels most heedful,
Recieve each mild spirit,
New worlds to inherit.

And there the lion's ruddy eyes
Shall flow with tears of gold:
And pitying the tender cries,
And walking round the fold:
Saying: "Wrath by his meekness
And by his health, sickness,
Is driven away,
From our immortal day.

"And now beside thee bleating lamb,
I can lie down and sleep;
Or think on him who bore thy name,
Grase after thee and weep.
For wash'd in life's river,
My bright mane for ever
Shall shine like the gold,
As I guard o'er the fold."

Recieve—*receive*
New worlds—*heaven*
there—*in heaven*
immortal day—*heaven's eternity*
lie down—*famous image from the Bible:*
    the lion will lie down beside the lamb
him—*Jesus, the lamb*
Grase—*Graze*
life's river—*river of purification*

19

NURSE'S SONG

The nursemaid tells of letting the children play through twilight—and of their joy.

When the voices of children are heard on the green
And laughing is heard on the hill,
My heart is at rest within my breast
And every thing else is still

"Then come home my children, the sun is gone down
And the dews of night arise;
Come come leave off play, and let us away
Till the morning appears in the skies."

"No no let us play, for it is yet day
And we cannot go to sleep;
Besides in the sky, the little birds fly
And the hills are all covered with sheep."

"Well well go & play till the light fades away
And then go home to bed."
The little ones leaped & shouted & laugh'd
And all the hills ecchoed.

Nurse's—*nursemaid's, babysitter's*
ecchoed—*echoed*

A DREAM

A dream about a lost ant—rescued by a firefly.
In the world of innocence, nature can be a realm
of caring and nurture.

Once a dream did weave a shade,
O'er my Angel-guarded bed,
That an Emmet lost its way
Where on grass methought I lay.

Troubled, wilderd and folorn;
Dark, benighted, travel-worn,
Over many a tangled spray
All heart-broke I heard her say:

"O my children! do they cry,
Do they hear their father sigh?
Now they look abroad to see,
Now return and weep for me."

Pitying I drop'd a tear:
But I saw a glow-worm near:
Who replied: "What wailing wight
Calls the watchman of the night?

"I am set to light the ground,
While the beetle goes his round:
Follow now the beetle's hum,
Little wanderer, hie thee home."

Shade—*dark imagination*

Emmet—*ant*

wilderd—*bewildered*

folorn—*forlorn*

benighted—*out at night*

spray—*branch*

glow-worm—*firefly, possibly the glowing female larva form*

hie thee—*get yourself*

ON ANOTHER'S SORROW

The speaker can't think of not sympathizing with others' sorrow; nor could a mother.
God, he decides, also must suffer with us and comfort us.

Can I see another's woe,
And not be in sorrow too?
Can I see another's grief,
And not seek for kind relief?

Can I see a falling tear,
And not feel my sorrow's share?
Can a father see his child
Weep, nor be with sorrow fill'd?

Can a mother sit and hear
An infant groan, an infant fear?
No no never can it be.
Never never can it be.

And can he who smiles on all
Hear the wren with sorrows small,
Hear the small bird's grief & care
Hear the woes that infants bear—

And not sit beside the nest
Pouring pity in their breast,
And not sit the cradle near
Weeping tear on infant's tear?

he—*God*
wren—*a small bird*

22

And not sit both night & day,
Wiping all our tears away?
O! no never can it be.
Never never can it be.

He doth give his joy to all.
He becomes an infant small.
He becomes a man of woe.
He doth feel the sorrow too.

Think not, thou canst sigh a sigh,
And thy maker is not by.
Think not, thou canst weep a tear,
And thy maker is not near.

O! he gives to us his joy,
That our grief he may destroy;
Till our grief is fled & gone
He doth sit by us and moan.

doth—*does*
man of woe—*a suffering Jesus*
maker—*God*

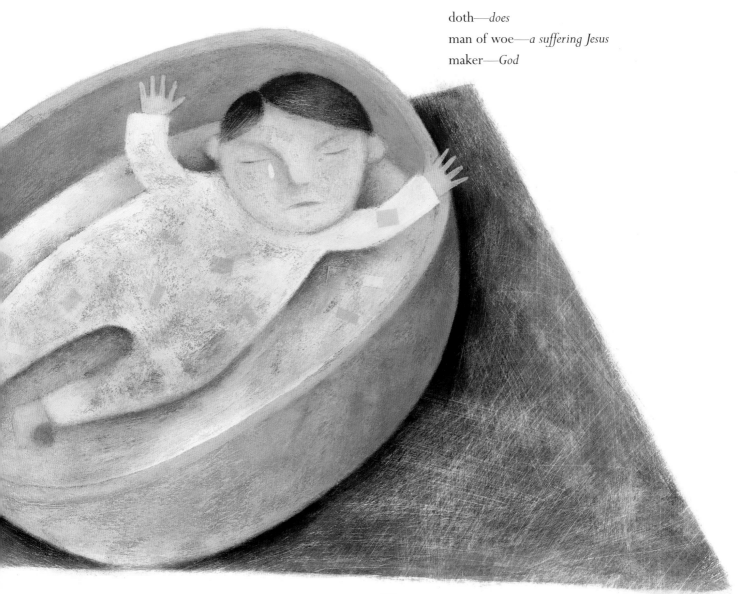

23

from *SONGS OF EXPERIENCE*

"Songs of Experience" offer the perspective of realistic insight and worldly knowledge, but also of disillusionment, criticism and, sometimes, cynicism.

THE CLOD & THE PEBBLE

The trodden Clod of Clay sings of selfless love; he is answered by an indestructible pebble who asserts that we use others only to please ourselves.

"Love seeketh not Itself to please,
Nor for itself hath any care;
But for another gives its ease,
And builds a Heaven in Hell's despair."

So sang a little Clod of Clay,
Trodden with the cattles feet:
But a Pebble of the brook,
Warbled out these metres meet:

"Love seeketh only Self to please,
To bind another to its delight;
Joys in another's loss of ease,
And builds a Hell in Heaven's despite.

Clod—*little piece of earth*
metres—*verses*
in despite—*showing spitefulness toward heaven*

HOLY THURSDAY

The speaker ironically observes the bad treatment given to charity children; they were required to march to St. Paul's Cathedral in London on a Thursday during Lent. He (or she) judges the rich country as one of moral poverty.

Is this a holy thing to see,
In a rich and fruitful land,
Babes reduced to misery,
Fed with cold and usurous hand?

Is that trembling cry a song?
Can it be a song of joy?
And so many children poor?
It is a land of poverty!

And their sun does never shine.
And their fields are bleak & bare.
And their ways are fill'd with thorns.
It is eternal winter there.

For where-e'er the sun does shine,
And where-e'er the rain does fall:
Babe can never hunger there
Nor poverty the mind appall.

usurous——*usurious: exacting,*
  demanding
where-e'er——*wherever*
appall——*cast a pall over, darken*

from THE LITTLE GIRL LOST

Little Lyca is lost in the desert overnight but finds friends among the wild animals.

In the southern clime,
Where the summer's prime,
Never fades away,
Lovely Lyca lay.

Seven summers old
Lovely Lyca told;
She had wanderd long,
Hearing wild birds' song.

"Sweet sleep come to me
Underneath this tree;
Do father, mother weep.—
'Where can Lyca sleep?'

"Lost in desart wild
Is your little child.
How can Lyca sleep,
If her mother weep?

"If her heart does ake,
Then let Lyca wake;
If my mother sleep,
Lyca shall not weep.

"Frowning frowning night,
O'er this desart bright,
Let thy moon arise,
While I close my eyes."

clime—*part of the world*
desart—*desert*

Sleeping Lyca lay:
While the beasts of prey,
Come from caverns deep,
View'd the maid asleep.

The kingly lion stood
And the virgin view'd,
Then he gambold round
O'er the hallowed ground:

Leopards, tygers play,
Round her as she lay;
While the lion old,
Bow'd his mane of gold.

virgin—*young girl*
gambold—*gamboled, leaped playfully*
hallowed—*sacred*

THE LITTLE GIRL FOUND

Lyca's parents seek her in hardship and are knocked down by a lion. But the lion turns out to be an angel and he takes them to Lyca. They all live in a dell among peaceful lions, wolves, and tigers. Is this heaven?

All the night in woe
Lyca's parents go:
Over vallies deep,
While the desarts weep.

Tired and woe-begone,
Hoarse with making moan:
Arm in arm seven days,
They trac'd the desert ways.

Seven nights they sleep,
Among shadows deep:
And dream they see their child
Starv'd in desart wild.

Pale thro' pathless ways
The fancied image strays,
Famish'd, weeping, weak
With hollow piteous shriek.

Rising from unrest,
The trembling woman prest
With feet of weary woe;
She could no further go.

In his arms he bore
Her arm'd with sorrow sore;
Till before their way,
A couching lion lay.

vallies—*valleys*
woe-begone—*overcome with grief*   prest—*pressed on*
desart—*desert*   arm'd—*covered*
fancied—*imagined*   couching—*lying*

Turning back was vain,
Soon his heavy mane,
Bore them to the ground;
Then he stalk'd around,

Smelling to his prey.
But their fears allay,
When he licks their hands;
And silent by them stands.

They look upon his eyes
Fill'd with deep surprise:
And wondering behold,
A spirit arm'd in gold.

On his head a crown
On his shoulders down,
Flow'd his golden hair.
Gone was all their care.

"Follow me," he said,
"Weep not for the maid;
In my palace deep,
Lyca lies asleep."

Then they followed,
Where the vision led:
And saw their sleeping child,
Among tygers wild.

To this day they dwell
In a lonely dell
Nor fear the wolvish howl,
Nor the lions' growl.

smelling to—*smelling*
allay—*go away*
spirit—*probably an angel—or Jesus, who
    was often portrayed with long golden hair*

tygers—*tigers*
dell—*a small, secluded valley; possibly
    heaven, where lion and lamb lie
    down together?*

THE CHIMNEY SWEEPER

The little chimney sweeper (compare this poem with the earlier one of the same name) explains that his parents put him in the sweeper's dark clothes and act as if everything is okay because he can seem happy. But he blames them, their God, priest, and king, whom they praise, for his sweeper's hard life away from the outdoors.

A little black thing among the snow:
Crying weep, weep, in notes of woe!
"Where are thy father & mother? say?"
"They are both gone up to the church to pray.

"Because I was happy upon the heath,
And smil'd among the winter's snow:
They clothed me in the clothes of death,
And taught me to sing the notes of woe.

"And because I am happy, & dance & sing,
They think they have done me no injury:
And are gone to praise God & his Priest & King
Who make up a heaven of our misery."

weep—*sweep, the street cry used by chimney sweepers*
    offering their services, but rightly sounds like weep
heath—*open, wild country with bushes*
clothes of death—*dark, formal clothes of chimney sweeps*
notes of woe—*the call, sweep, sweep (weep, weep)*
make up a heaven of—*build a heaven on*

NURSE'S SONG

This nursemaid turns green with envy seeing the children at play, forces them to come home, and chides them harshly.

When the voices of children are heard on the green
And whisprings are in the dale:
The days of my youth rise fresh in my mind,
My face turns green and pale.

"Then come home my children, the sun is gone down
And the dews of night arise
Your spring & your day, are wasted in play
And your winter and night in disguise."

green—*public playfield*
dale—*valley*
green—*color for envy*
disguise—*false shows and games?*

THE SICK ROSE

The narrator seems to mock the rose about the worm that flew secretly into its center and is destroying it. The poem tempts us to find meanings for humans but doesn't tell us which are right, if any.

O Rose thou art sick.
The invisible worm
That flies in the night,
In the howling storm:

Has found out thy bed
Of crimson joy:
And his dark secret love
Does thy life destroy.

THE ANGEL

The speaker tells a dream: she was a queen guarded by an angel. She insisted on weeping and didn't tell him her delight. He left. She armed herself to the teeth. When he came again she was armed, and she was growing old. The dream makes us think about how we may keep people at a distance as time goes by.

I Dreamt a Dream! what can it mean?
And that I was a maiden Queen:
Guarded by an Angel mild;
Witless woe, was ne'er beguil'd!

And I wept both night and day
And he wip'd my tears away
And I wept both day and night
And hid from him my heart's delight.

So he took his wings and fled:
Then the morn blush'd rosy red:
I dried my tears & armd my fears
With ten thousand shields and spears.

Soon my Angel came again:
I was arm'd, he came in vain:
For the time of youth was fled
And grey hairs were on my head.

maiden—*unmarried*
Witless woe . . .—*foolish grief was never
    diverted (beguil'd)*
red—*usually a bad sign in the morning*

THE TYGER

Who dared to make the fierce and wonderful tiger? Was it God—the same who made the Lamb? In Blake's illustration the tiger looks, surprisingly, not very fierce, like a big pussycat.

Tyger, Tyger, burning bright,
In the forests of the night:
What immortal hand or eye,
Could frame thy fearful symmetry?

In what distant deeps or skies
Burnt the fire of thine eyes?
On what wings dare he aspire?
What the hand dare sieze the fire?

And what shoulder, & what art,
Could twist the sinews of thy heart?
And when thy heart began to beat,
What dread hand? & what dread feet?

What the hammer? what the chain?
In what furnace was thy brain?
What the anvil? what dread grasp,
Dare its deadly terrors clasp?

When the stars threw down their spears
And water'd heaven with their tears:
Did he smile his work to see?
Did he who made the Lamb make thee?

Tyger, Tyger, burning bright,
In the forests of the night:
What immortal hand or eye,
Dare frame thy fearful symmetry?

Tyger—*tiger*
night—*dark forests*
frame—*produce*
symmetry—*balanced order*
deeps—*valleys, oceans?*
aspire—*rise up*
sieze—*seize*

sinews—*muscles*
dread—*dreadful, powerful*
stars—*fallen angels becoming devils*
tears—*at falling from God*
he—*God?*
Lamb—*the animal, and possibly also Jesus, Lamb of God*

34

AH! SUN-FLOWER

The sunflower seeks a world beyond this one, presumably that of the sun—the same place that unfulfilled people seek to go to after death.

Ah Sun-flower! weary of time,
Who countest the steps of the Sun:
Seeking after that sweet golden clime
Where the traveller's journey is done.

Where the Youth pined away with desire,
And the pale Virgin shrouded in snow:
Arise from their graves and aspire,
Where my Sun-flower wishes to go.

clime—*place*
aspire—*desire to be*

THE GARDEN OF LOVE

The happy garden of love has a new building: a chapel. And the garden has been wasted, flowers replaced by gravestones, and priests making rounds like guards prohibiting joy and desires.

I went to the Garden of Love,
And saw what I never had seen:
A Chapel was built in the midst,
Where I used to play on the green.

And the gates of this Chapel were shut,
And Thou shalt not writ over the door;
So I turn'd to the Garden of Love,
That so many sweet flowers bore,

And I saw it was filled with graves,
And tomb-stones where flowers should be:
And Priests in black gowns, were walking their rounds,
And binding with briars, my joys & desires.

green—*public park*

thou shalt not—*the Commandments, here turned into
    something merely negative*

INFANT SORROW

The difficult baby came into a sad and dangerous world; he strove against his father and, tired, grudgingly lay on his mother's breast.

My mother groand! my father wept.
Into the dangerous world I leapt:
Helpless, naked, piping loud:
Like a fiend hid in a cloud.

Struggling in my father's hands:
Striving against my swadling bands:
Bound and weary I thought best
To sulk upon my mother's breast.

groand—*groaned*
dangerous—*perilous: so it
  seemed to him*
fiend—*devil, evil spirit*
swadling bands—*swaddling
  clothes: strips of linen
  wound around infants*

A POISON TREE

The speaker did not explain his anger to his enemy, as he had to his friend. He (or she) nursed it and it grew into a tree. He is happy to find his enemy has stolen an apple and died from it.

I was angry with my friend:
I told my wrath, my wrath did end.
I was angry with my foe:
I told it not, my wrath did grow.

And I waterd it in fears,
Night & morning with my tears:
And I sunned it with smiles,
And with soft deceitful wiles.

And it grew both day and night.
Till it bore an apple bright.
And my foe beheld it shine,
And he knew that it was mine.

And into my garden stole.
When the night had veild the pole;
In the morning glad I see
My foe outstretchd beneath the tree.

wiles—*tricks*

veild the pole—*covered
the sky*

A LITTLE BOY LOST

The little boy is executed for stating that no one loves someone more than himself, or can think of someone greater, or can love his father more than he does. The speaker asks if this can really be happening here, in England.

"Nought loves another as itself
Nor venerates another so.
Nor is it possible to Thought
A greater than itself to know:

"And Father, how can I love you,
Or any of my brothers more?
I love you like the little bird
That picks up crumbs around the door."

The Priest sat by and heard the child.
In trembling zeal he siez'd his hair:
He led him by his little coat:
And all admir'd the Priestly care.

And standing on the altar high,
"Lo what a fiend is here!" said he:
"One who sets reason up for judge
Of our most holy Mystery."

The weeping child could not be heard.
The weeping parents wept in vain:
They strip'd him to his little shirt,
And bound him in an iron chain.

And burn'd him in a holy place,
Where many had been burn'd before:
The weeping parents wept in vain.
Are such things done on Albion's shore?

Nought—*no one* Mystery—*religious belief*
siez'd—*seized* strip'd—*stripped*
fiend—*demon, devil* Albions—*England's*

THE SCHOOL-BOY

The schoolboy hates school in the summer. He advocates childhood joy to prepare for life's later hardships. Blake understandably was uncertain if this poem should go under Innocence or Experience.

I love to rise in a summer morn,
When the birds sing on every tree;
The distant huntsman winds his horn,
And the sky-lark sings with me.
O! what sweet company.

But to go to school in a summer morn,
O! it drives all joy away:
Under a cruel eye outworn,
The little ones spend the day,
In sighing and dismay.

Ah! then at times I drooping sit,
And spend many an anxious hour.
Nor in my book can I take delight,
Nor sit in learning's bower,
Worn thro' with the dreary shower.

How can the bird that is born for joy,
Sit in a cage and sing?
How can a child when fears annoy,
But droop his tender wing,
And forget his youthful spring?

winds—*plays (puts wind into but often
   pronounced as winds—a clock)*
sky-lark—*a song bird*
learning's bower—*secluded study area*
shower—*of school work? or just rain?*
annoy—*bother, upset*

O! father & mother, if buds are nip'd,
And blossoms blown away,
And if the tender plants are strip'd
Of their joy in the springing day,
By sorrow and care's dismay,

How shall the summer arise in joy?
Or the summer fruits appear?
Or how shall we gather what griefs destroy?
Or bless the mellowing year,
When the blasts of winter appear?

nip'd—*nipped*
strip'd—*stripped*
springing—*opening spring of life*
summer—*of life*
mellowing year—*maturity*
winter—*old age*

from THE MARRIAGE OF HEAVEN AND HELL

This strange book includes what the narrator heard from angels and devils. This first section is from his summary of the argument, which asserts the necessity of differences and implies that hell has value as a place of energy, which has been called evil.

Without Contraries is no progression. Attraction and Repulsion, Reason and Energy, Love and Hate, are necessary to Human existence.

From these contraries spring what the religious call Good & Evil. Good is the passive that obeys Reason. Evil is the active springing from Energy.

Good is Heaven. Evil is Hell.

* * *

This section is a group of Proverbs the narrator says he obtained, evidently from the devils, when he visited hell. They are hard sayings to work out; they force us to think and rethink.

The fox provides for himself, but God provides for the lion.

Think in the morning, Act in the noon, Eat in the evening, Sleep in the night.

He who has sufferd you to impose on him knows you.

As the plow follows words, so God rewards prayers.

The tygers of wrath are wiser than the horses of instruction.

Expect poison from the standing water.

You never know what is enough unless you know what is more than enough.

Listen to the fools reproach! it is a kingly title!

The eyes of fire, the nostrils of air, the mouth of water, the beard of earth.

The weak in courage is strong in cunning.

The apple tree never asks the beech how he shall grow, nor the lion the horse how he shall take his prey.

The thankful reciever bears a plentiful harvest.

If others had not been foolish, we should be so.

The soul of sweet delight can never be defil'd.

When thou seest an Eagle, thou seest a portion of Genius; lift up thy head!

As the catterpiller chooses the fairest leaves to lay her eggs on, so the priest lays his curse on the fairest joys.

To create a little flower is the labour of ages.

Contraries—*oppositions*	sufferd—*suffered, allowed*	reciever—*receiver*
fox—*known for cleverness*	plow—*does the plow follow words?*	bears—*receives?*
lion—*known for bravery*	tygers—*tigers*	catterpiller—*caterpillar*

* * *

The narrator says he has a friend, formerly an angel, now a devil. He then gives this famous rule.

One Law for the Lion & Ox is Oppression

Oppression—*unjust control*

from *Jerusalem: The Emanation of the Giant Albion*

This exclamation by Los to his spectre and the description of the effect on the spectre is from one of Blake's many epics, also called prophetic books. Los, the hero—blacksmith and artist—works unremittingly and against great forces of despair and evil, to revive the giant Albion, representing England, which Blake felt was in dire straits.

"I must Create a System, or be enslav'd by another Man's.
I will not Reason & Compare: my business is to Create."

So Los, in fury & strength: in indignation & burning wrath.
Shuddring the Spectre howls, his howlings terrify the night.
He stamps around the Anvil, beating blows of stern despair
He curses Heaven & Earth, Day & Night & Sun & Moon
He curses Forest Spring & River, Desart & sandy Waste
Cities & Nations, Families & Peoples, Tongues & Laws,
Driven to desperation by Los's terrors & threatning fears.

Jerusalem—*Blake's spiritual home*
Emanation—*better self coming forth, his
    positive side*
Giant Albion—*giant representing
    Albion—a literary name for England*
System—*ordering scheme, for Blake
    usually myth*
so Los—*thus spoke Los, the hero blacksmith*
Spectre—*a phantom of himself that impedes
    his creative work; he carries on here after
    hearing Los*
Anvil—*blacksmith's metal block for
    hammering on*
Desart—*desert, wild place*
Tongues—*languages*

44

from AUGURIES OF INNOCENCE

This poem continues exploring the innocent's perception, showing how the world is seen by innocence—in an endearing but also exceptional concern for all things.

To see a World in a Grain of Sand
And a Heaven in a Wild Flower:
Hold Infinity in the palm of your hand
And Eternity in an hour.
A Robin Red breast in a Cage
Puts all Heaven in a Rage.
A dove house filld with doves & Pigeons
Shudders Hell thro all its regions.
A dog starvd at his Master's Gate
Predicts the ruin of the State.
A Horse misusd upon the Road
Calls to Heaven for Human blood.
Each outcry of the hunted Hare
A fibre from the Brain does tear.
A Skylark wounded in the wing,
A Cherubim does cease to sing.
The Game Cock clipd & armd for fight
Does the Rising Sun affright.
Every Wolf's & Lion's howl
Raises from Hell a Human Soul.
The wild deer wandring here & there
Keeps the Human Soul from Care.
The Lamb misusd breeds Public strife
And yet forgives the Butcher's Knife.

Auguries—*readings of signs, here perceptions
of the relations of things*
thro—*through*
Cherubim—*angels (Blake uses as a singular)*
Game Cock—*rooster trained for cockfighting*
affright—*frighten*

from *MILTON*

This song is a selection from the Preface to another of Blake's many long, epic poems or prophetic books. Blake portrays himself as making contact with the seventeenth-century poet John Milton, a great spirit in Blake's vision of him.

And did those feet in ancient time
Walk upon England's mountains green:
And was the holy Lamb of God,
On England's pleasant pastures seen!

And did the Countenance Divine,
Shine forth upon our clouded hills?
And was Jerusalem builded here,
Among these dark Satanic Mills?

Bring me my Bow of burning gold:
Bring me my Arrows of desire:
Bring me my Spear: O clouds unfold!
Bring me my Chariot of fire!

I will not cease from Mental Fight,
Nor shall my Sword sleep in my hand:
Till we have built Jerusalem,
In England's green & pleasant Land.

Lamb of God—*Jesus, but here applied to the (for Blake) Jesus-like Milton*
Countenance Divine—*divine face, again comparing Milton to divinity*
Jerusalem—*capitol of ancient Israel, here a holy city, perhaps of Milton's mind or work*
satanic mills—*hellish mills, could be actual mills of Blake's time or overly rational systems of thought*
Mental Fight—*inner battle, to see things right?*
sword—*when ancient Jerusalem was rebuilt the builders carried swords for protection*

from To Thomas Butts, October 2, 1800

Blake included a poem in a letter to his friend, who bought many of his illustrations.
He was staying in the country and writes of his special perceptions there.

To my Friend Butts I write
My first Vision of Light.
On the yellow sands sitting
The Sun was Emitting
His Glorious beams
From Heaven's high Streams.
Over Sea, over Land
My Eyes did Expand
Into regions of air
Away from all Care,
Into regions of fire
Remote from Desire.
The Light of the Morning
Heaven's Mountains adorning
In particles bright
The jewels of Light
Distinct shone & clear.
Amazd & in fear
I each particle gazed,
Astonishd, Amazed;
For each was a Man
Human formd. Swift I ran,
For they beckond to me
Remote by the Sea,
Saying: "Each grain of Sand,
Every Stone on the Land,
Each rock & each hill,
Each fountain & rill,
Each herb & each tree,
Mountain, hill, earth & sea,
Cloud, Meteor & Star,
Are Men Seen Afar."

particle—*of sand*
each—*each particle of sand*
afar—*from a distance*

47

INDEX

"Ah! Sun-Flower," 35

"Angel, The," 33

"Auguries of Innocence," 45

Blake, William

    Blake, Catherine (wife), 5-6

    born, 6, 40

    brother, 5

    engraver, 7

    father, 6

    soldier, 5

"Chimney Sweeper, The," in *Songs of Innocence,* 14

"Chimney Sweeper, The," in *Songs of Experience,* 30

"Clod & the Pebble, The," 24

"Divine Image, The," 17

"Dream, A," 21

"Ecchoing Green, The," 11

"Garden of Love, The,"36

"Holy Thursday," 25

"Infant Sorrow," 37

Jerusalem: The Emanation of the Giant Albion, 44

"Lamb, The," 12

Leonardo da Vinci, 7

"Little Boy Found, The," 16

"Little Boy Lost, A," 39

"Little Boy Lost, The," 15

"Little Girl Found, The," 28

"Little Girl Lost, The," 26

Los, 8, 9, 44

Marriage of Heaven and Hell, The, 42

Michelangelo, 7

Milton, 46

Milton, John, 7, 46

"Night," 18

"Nurse's Song," in *Songs of Innocence,* 20

"Nurse's Song," in *Songs of Experience,* 31

"On Another's Sorrow," 22

Orc, 8

Paradise Lost, 7

"Poison Tree, A," 38

Raphael, 7

Romantic poets, 6

"School Boy, The," 40

"Shepherd, The," 10

"Sick Rose," 32

Song of Los, The, 8

Songs of Innocence, 6, 8, 10–23

Songs of Innocence and Songs of Experience, 8

Songs of Experience, 7, 8, 24–41

To Thomas Butts, October 2, 1800, 47

"Tyger, The," 34

Urizen, 8, 9